AUSTRALIA'S REMARKABLE WILDLIFE

JOHN LESLEY

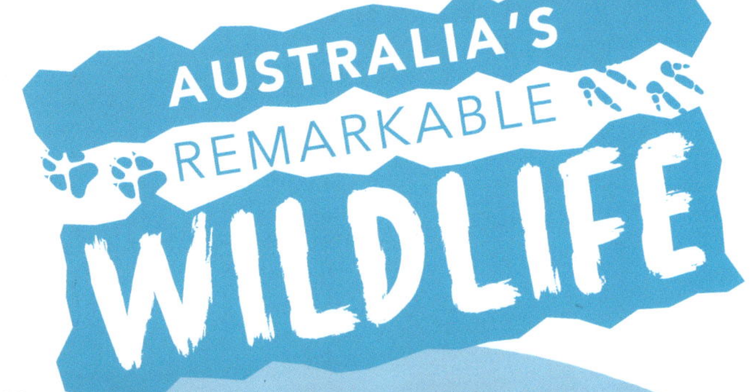

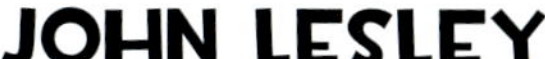

KOOKABURRA

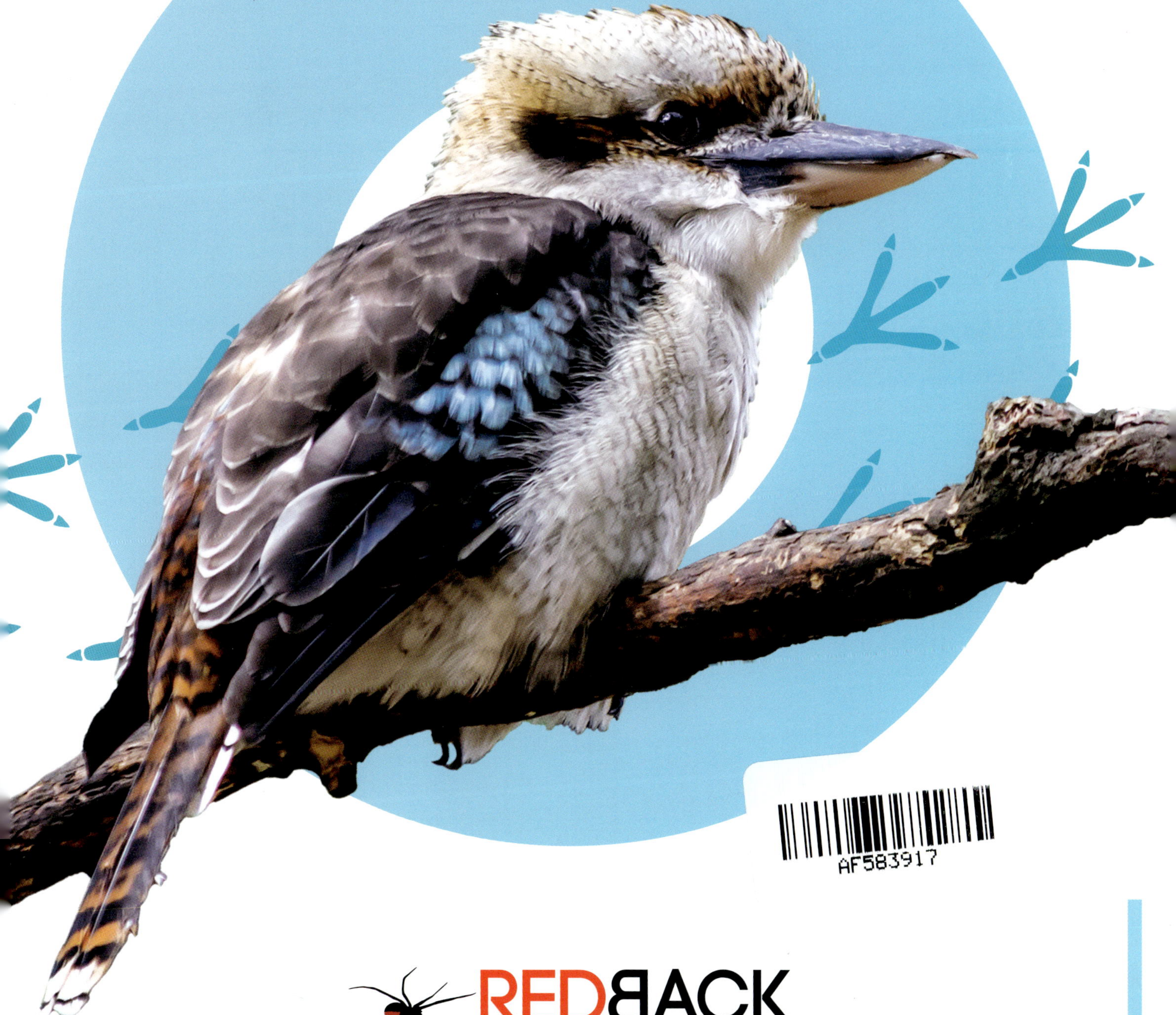

REDBACK publishing

First Published 2026 by
Redback Publishing
Suite 6, 13a Narabang Way,
Belrose NSW 2085
Australia

www.redbackpublishing.com
orders@redbackpublishing.com

ISBN 978-1-761400-85-8

A catalogue record for this book is available from the National Library of Australia

Author: John Lesley
Editing: Words at Work
Design: Redback Publishing

Original illustrations © Redback Publishing 2026
Originated by Redback Publishing

Acknowledgements
Abbreviations: l—left, r—right, b—bottom, t—top, c—centre, m—middle. We would like to thank the following for permission to reproduce photographs: Images © shutterstock; p8cl map distribution Aa77zz, CC0, via Wikimedia Commons; p9tl Greg Miles from Australia, CC BY-SA 2.0 (https://creativecommons.org/licenses/by-sa/2.0), via Wikimedia Commons; p9tr Doug Janson, CC BY-SA 3.0 (https://creativecommons.org/licenses/by-sa/3.0), via Wikimedia Commons); p21c film strip frame 1, Numa Pictures Corporation, Public domain, via Wikimedia Commons; p21c film strip frame 2, TCM, Public domain, via Wikimedia Commons; p21c film strip frame 3, trailer screenshot (MGM), Public domain, via Wikimedia Commons; p21c film strip frame 4, MGM, Public domain, via Wikimedia Commons; p21c film strip frame 5, trailer screenshot (MGM), Public domain, via Wikimedia Commons; p21c film strip frame 6, Public domain, via Wikimedia Commons

CONTENTS

KOOKABURRA

The laughing kookaburra is an Australian icon. Its call and its confident manner make it one of the most loved and easily recognised birds in Australia.

Feathers raised on head
Dark stripe behind eyes
Excellent eyesight

KOOKABURRA BASIC FACTS

KINGFISHERS AND KOOKABURRAS

The kookaburra is a type of bird called a kingfisher, although it rarely takes fish out of waterways. There are a few different types of kookaburras, but the laughing kookaburra of eastern Australia is the one that most people think of when they hear the name.

EMBLEM

The laughing kookaburra is the official bird emblem of the Australian state of New South Wales. It is also used by many clubs and groups on their logos and in their advertising.

The kookaburra is a large bird, and the biggest kingfisher in the world. Kookaburras can grow up to 50 centimetres long from the tip of the beak to the end of the tail, and can weigh up to half a kilogram.

APPEARANCE

Kookaburras are covered in brown and white feathers, with some having small patches of blue and orange feathers as well. They have a pale-coloured breast and a dark stripe near the eyes. The large beak has a tiny but sharp hook at the tip that is used to catch their prey. They also have sharp claws.

KOOKABURRA NAMES

The kookaburra's name is based on a Wiradjuri word, and it refers to the noisy sound that is the bird's call.

KOOKABURRAS IN AUSTRALIA

The laughing kookaburra of eastern Australia is the best-known species, but there are also other types of kookaburra that live in Australia and on the island of New Guinea.

The scientific name of the laughing kookaburra is *Dacelo novaeguineae*

In northern Australia, there is a blue-winged kookaburra with the scientific name *Dacelo leachii*

Spangled kookaburra (*Dacelo tyro*)

Rufous-bellied kookaburra (*Dacelo gaudichaud*)

KOOKABURRAS ON THE ISLAND OF NEW GUINEA

Three species of kookaburra live on the islands of New Guinea:

1) Shovel-billed kookaburra (*Dacelo rex*)
2) Spangled kookaburra (*Dacelo tyro*)
3) Rufous-bellied kookaburra (*Dacelo gaudichaud*)

Shovel-billed kookaburra (*Dacelo rex*)

DO KOOKABURRAS REALLY LAUGH?

ICONIC LAUGH

The different species of kookaburra all have different calls, but the eastern laughing kookaburra is the one with the iconic laugh. In addition to their loud, laughter-like call, they also have a bold, confident manner. They will sit on a tree branch staring down at people, waiting to see if any scraps of food are available. When they suddenly start to laugh loudly, it is tempting to imagine they are making fun of humans!

FAMILY FUN

When they are together, a family of kookaburras will make a variety of other noises to communicate with each other. They chuckle, hiccup and chatter with each other, and can be very quiet or very loud.

When you hear the laughing call ringing through the bush, there is no mistaking it for anything other than a kookaburra letting every other bird in the area know that it owns the territory all around.

KOOKABURRA ADAPTATIONS

BEAK, EYES AND CLAWS

Kookaburras have a large beak and keen eyesight that they need to catch their prey. Their sharp claws help them hold onto a wriggling small animal until they can kill it.

UHD 3...2...1...0...1...2...3 00:35:02

FEATHERS

The brown and grey feathers enable a kookaburra to camouflage itself, which is a protection against predators and a way to watch prey without being spotted.

COMMUNICATING

The loud, laughing call is used to proclaim their territory and to let a potential mate know where they are.

FLOCKS

Kookaburras are highly social birds and often live in extended family groups composed of the adult breeding pair as well as offspring that remain in the same territory as helpers. The family group helps to feed and protect the chicks. They all spend much of their time high up on a gumtree branch, or on power lines, constantly scanning the ground for prey.

KOOKABURRA HABITAT

The laughing kookaburra lives in the eucalyptus forests, woodlands and grasslands of eastern Australia. They are also common in parks and gardens in suburban areas.

GARDENS

Although kookaburras are kingfishers, they do not usually take fish from creeks and lakes as other kingfishers do. Despite this, gardeners sometimes complain that a kookaburra has completely emptied all the goldfish out of their garden pond.

Because they need high perches from which to survey the ground for food, the presence of power poles and other tall structures in suburban areas is an advantage for kookaburras, as they will use them when there are no tree branches.

Kookaburras need tree hollows for nesting. Keeping large old trees in new suburbs is important if kookaburras are to continue to live there too. Just planting lots of new trees is not enough, as it will take decades for the young trees to develop hollows that can be used for nests.

KOOKABURRA LIFECYCLE

The lifecycle of a kookaburra starts when a female lays about three eggs in a tree hollow or a similar location. Kookaburras might dig a hole out of a large termite nest high up in a tree if there are not enough tree hollows to use for nesting. Both the male and female care for the eggs and chicks.

Kookaburras use termite nests as nests for their eggs

It is usual for the strongest chicks to kill the weakest ones in the nest. While this seems harsh, it is nature's way of favouring the strongest offspring for the eventual benefit of the whole species.

NEW START

When the older family members are ready to mate and have their own chicks, they usually move away and claim their own territories.

FAMILY SUPPORT

Other older family members also help raise and care for the chicks. This is a behavioural adaptation that helps ensure the survival of the offspring. Even in the relative safety of a treetop hollow, the chicks can be taken by snakes, climbing goannas, feral cats and birds of prey during the day and night. The more helpers there are to keep watch, the better the chances of survival for the new generation.

KOOKABURRA FOOD CHAIN

WHAT DOES A KOOKABURRA EAT?

Kookaburras feed on a variety of prey, including insects, worms, snakes, lizards, fish and small mammals. The eastern Australian laughing kookaburra has been introduced into Western Australia, Tasmania and New Zealand because of its reputation for controlling the numbers of snakes, rats and mice.

A kookaburra will sit motionless on a branch, scanning the ground for anything that moves and is edible. When they spot something moving, they silently swoop down and grab it, shake it to kill it and then eat it whole. If the prey animal is too big to kill quickly on the ground, the kookaburra will take it back up into a tree, bash it against a branch to kill it, and eat it there in safety from ground-dwelling predators.

WHAT EATS KOOKABURRAS?

Kookaburras are large and strong and will fight a predator with their beak and claws. Kookaburra chicks are sometimes eaten by goannas, large lizards, eagles, snakes and feral cats and dogs.

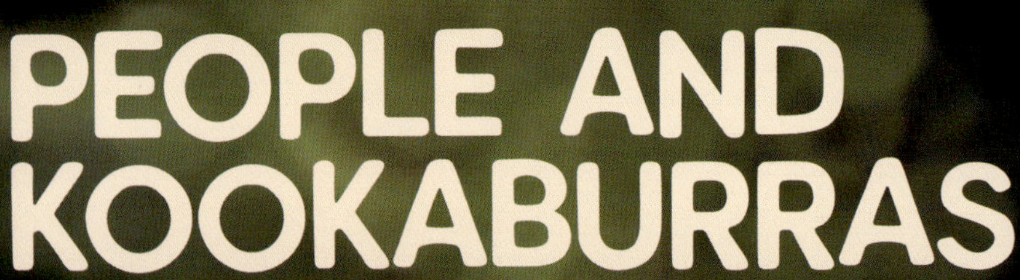

PEOPLE AND KOOKABURRAS

Kookaburras are easily tamed when offered meat, but giving them treats with too much fat and not enough bones and skin tends to make kookaburras sick.

Kookaburras are often seen in parks and gardens in suburban areas, where they are happy to come close to people if there is a possibility of a handout of food. Sometimes, a wild kookaburra will bypass a human offer and simply fly down to a barbecue and steal a whole steak.

RAIN IS COMING!

Farmers in Australia will tell you that they know when rain is coming because the kookaburras start laughing in the middle of the day, instead of only in the morning and evening.

KOOKABURRAS IN MOVIES

For decades, the movie industry in the United States has used the kookaburra laugh as a sound effect for movies set in the jungles of Africa and South America, where the kookaburra does not live. No other bird in the world sounds like a laughing kookaburra, so hearing one in a movie set in a non-Australian location always amuses Australian audiences.

ARE KOOKABURRAS ENDANGERED?

The laughing kookaburra is not currently under threat of extinction. They are big enough to fight off attacks by the currawongs, crows and noisy miners that have driven most of the smaller birds away from suburban areas of the Australian east coast. People who hand-feed wildlife will often find all four of these larger types of birds lined up on their balcony railing, patiently waiting for some food.

With more and more trees being felled to provide housing for Australia's growing human needs, the nesting sites for kookaburras are also being destroyed. Balancing the needs of human families with the needs of kookaburras is difficult.

KOOKABURRA QUESTIONS AND ANSWERS

Q. Why do kookaburras laugh?

A. They laugh to let other kookaburras know that they have claimed all the territory around them for their own family.

Q. Do kookaburras ever attack people?

A. If you were to climb a tree to get a look at their nest, they are likely to try to drive you away.

Q.
How do I encourage kookaburras to come to my garden?

A.
Kookaburras need tall old trees for nests. They also need lizards and bugs to eat. Feeding them too much food from your kitchen is likely to eventually make them sick.

Q.
Do they fly in flocks?

A.
Kookaburras live together in small family groups, but they do not fly around in huge flocks. The male and female birds probably mate for life. Offspring stay with them for up to a few years, before moving away to start their own families.

AUSTRALIAN KINGFISHERS

The kookaburra is a kingfisher and is related to many other species of kingfisher that live in Australia.

Azure kingfisher (*Ceyx azureus*)

Collared kingfisher (*Todiramphus chloris*)

Buff-breasted paradise kingfisher (*Tanysiptera sylvia*)

Red-backed kingfisher (Todiramphus pyrrhopygius)
4K UHD
Forest kingfisher (Todiramphus macleayii)
Sacred kingfisher (Todiramphus sanctus)
4K UHD
00:35:02

SORTING ANIMALS INTO GROUPS

Biologists divide all living things around the world into groups. They call this process classification.

The two basic groups of animals are called:

VERTEBRATES

Vertebrates have a backbone

INVERTEBRATES

Invertebrates do not have a backbone

Vertebrates are further divided into these groups (classes). Kookaburras are birds and belong in the class called Aves.

CAN I KEEP A KOOKABURRA AS A PET?

It is illegal to keep a kookaburra as a pet in Australia. Kookaburras have very special needs, and they have evolved to look after themselves in the wild.

Keeping a kookaburra in a cage would probably lead to it becoming ill and unhappy.

If you care about kookaburras, take an interest in preserving their bush habitats so they can continue to laugh at us whenever they want to.

GLOSSARY

camouflage disguise something by making it appear to blend with the surroundings

emblem symbol

extended family including family members beyond the parents and current children

felled cut down

iconic widely known as a symbol of something

mate stay together to breed young

nestling baby bird in a nest

offspring young of an animal

proclaim announce loudly

scanning looking around carefully

INDEX